W9-ANJ-697

MEL BAY PRESENTS

STUDENT PIANO CLASSICS

QWIKGUIDE®

1 2 3 4 5 6 7 8 9 0

© 2006 BY MEL BAY PUBLICATIONS, INC., PACIFIC, MO 63069.
ALL RIGHTS RESERVED. INTERNATIONAL COPYRIGHT SECURED. B.M.I. MADE AND PRINTED IN U.S.A.
No part of this publication may be reproduced in whole or in part, or stored in a retrieval system, or transmitted in any form or by any means, electronic, mechanical, photocopy, recording, or otherwise, without written permission of the publisher.

Visit us on the Web at www.melbay.com – E-mail us at email@melbay.com

Contents

Aria

Bach was born in the little town of Eisenach, Germany, on the 21st day of March, 1685. With at least fifty musical relatives in his family it is no wonder that he took to music as soon as he could talk.

Bach's whole life was devoted to music. He was intensely religious and music, to him, was a means of worship.

The following piece is one of many which Bach wrote as teaching material for his children.

Prelude

Bach's earliest instruction in music was from an elder brother. The lessons were probably on the harpsichord, which was a common household instrument of the period. The young Bach's progress was undoubtedly rapid.

Preludes, in general, are written in a rather free form, somewhat in the style of an improvisation. Bach wrote many preludes, often using them as a first movement in suites, both instrumental and orchestral.

4
1
1 2
5
5

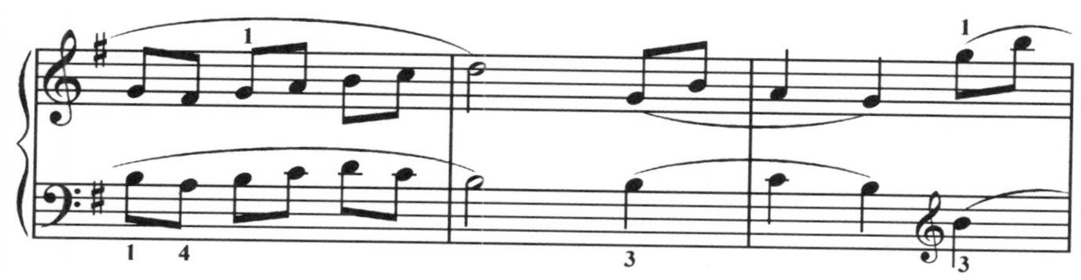
1
1
1 4
3
3

5
3 2 5
3
5
2
1

3 2 5
3
5
4
2
3
4
1 2
1
5
2

Song of Cherubino

Imagine being able to write a symphony when you were eight years old! Mozart did. It is in the key of E flat major and has three complete movements. It is scored for oboes, two French horns and strings (violins, violas, cellos and basses). One would never guess from listening to it that the composer was a child.

This "Song of Cherubino" is an air from Mozart's opera, The Marriage of Figaro.

Chorale Melody #60

Johann Forkel, who was the first person to write a biography of Bach, gives some interesting details regarding Bach as a teacher. In part he says: "He was the most instructive, clear and definite teacher that has ever been. In teaching the clavier (keyboard instruments), he began with simple exercises to develop the sympathetic touch, which was his distinction. When this elementary foundation had been laid, he allowed them to study his larger works."

After an extremely active career, Bach died on July 28, 1750, at the age of 66, a man who today is remembered as one of the greatest musicians of all time.

Minuet

(from String Trio in G major)

This piece was originally written by Mozart for two violins and cello.

Above measure 25, at the change of key, is the word TRIO. The word used in this sense means "contrasting section" and is applied with this meaning in minuets, marches, and Scherzos. In earlier times, there was a convention to write such sections strictly in three parts, but that practice has long ceased to be obligatory.

Trio
Fine

p
f
p
f
f
3
Minuet D.C.

A Graceful Minuet

This little minuet was written when Mozart was about seven years old.

Mozart's father once mentioned in a letter that as a child and boy, Wolfgang was too serious even to be childish, and that when sitting at the harpsichord or doing anything in the shape of music, he would not stand for a joke from anyone.

Ox Minuet

The full name of this composer is Franz Joseph Haydn, but he preferred to use his middle name, Joseph. He was born in Austria in 1732. His father was a master wheelwright, his mother a hired cook in the household of a count.

"Ox Minuet" is a sort of nick-name that has been given this piece to differentiate it from the many other minuets that Haydn wrote.

un poco cresc.
mf

cresc.

f
mf

f

Romance

(Op. 40)

Beethoven's early musical training consisted not only of lessons in piano but violin, viola and organ as well. Though his first teachers had no particular distinction, he learned much that would be helpful later in writing music for stringed instruments.

In 1781, when Beethoven was eleven years of age, he became the pupil of Christian Gottob Neefe. Neefe was an excellent teacher of piano and organ. Master and pupil had a high regard for each other, and Beethoven made astounding progress in his musical studies.

This piece was originally written for solo violin with orchestral accompaniment. The principal theme and development is included in this piano transcription.

mf
mp
mf
mf
mp
Fine
(Small notes optional)

This page has been left blank to avoid awkward page turns.

Andante

This piece was written by the child Mozart, perhaps when he was six or seven years of age. Its beauty lies in its simplicity of style and interesting harmonization. Notice how the lower notes for the left hand, measures 1 through 4, keep moving upward step by step until B flat is reached at the end of the line, while the melody above pursues its own course.

Minuet (G major)

In its earliest form the minuet consisted of two eight measure phrases each of which was repeated. This minuet is based on that form. It should be noted that Bach adds a second section, beginning with measure 17, which has the same number of measures as the first section (16 measures).

It is rather interesting to note that the melody of this minuet was once used as the basis for a popular song.

Sonatina in G Major

Unlike Mozart or Beethoven, the two other truly great composers of the Classic period, Haydn lived a long, successful and financially secure life. In 1761, when Haydn was 29 years of age, he received the appointment of Kapellmeister (leader-conductor) to the royal household of Prince Esterházy, a post he held until his death at the age of 77. His principal duties were to conduct the orchestra, chorus, and solo singers, all of whom lived at the estate, and to write musical compositions.

The following Sonatina is ideally suited for introducing the student to the form, style, and the technique of the sonata of the Classic period.

I

f
mp
p
cresc.
mf
mf

p
mp
mf
mf
f
mf

II

Minuet (♩ = 108)

III

IV

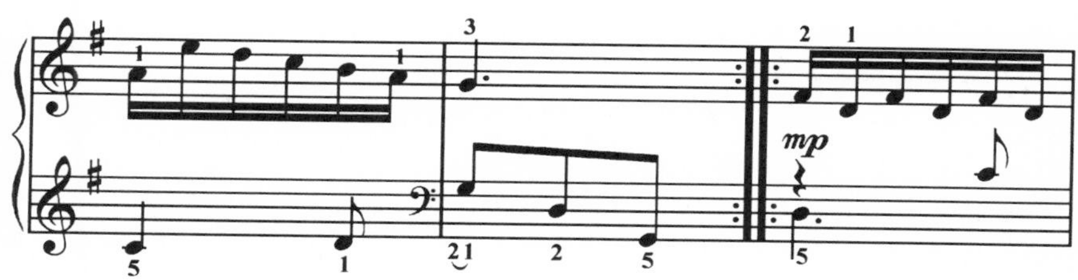

mf
f
mf
cresc.
f

Kontretanz

(Country Dance)

This short piece is from a collection of little pieces from the so-called *London Notebook*, written by the young Mozart between 1764-65. Notice the "foot stomps" marked with accents in measures 10 and 12. Be sure to accent these chords to emphasize the rural character of the piece.

Sonatina

Moderato
1
3 2
5
4 2
1
3
mp
2
4
1
5
5

4 5
3 2
1
1
4 3
5
3
mf
cresc.
5 2 4 2 5 1 2 1
5 1 2 1
2 4 2
3
1

1
5
mp
1
2
5
3 5
2

1
5
1 2
1
5
1 2
1
5
1 2
mf
mp
p
2 5
1
1
1
5

mp
mf
cresc.
mf

Chorale Melody #12

Waltz of the Flowers

Peter Ilyich Tchaikovsky, Russian composer, was born in Petrograd on May 7, 1840. Both of his parents were non-musical, a rare circumstance in the career of a world famous musician. Though piano lessons were part of his training from childhood onward, he was not encouraged to take up music as a profession. Instead he was trained to be a lawyer and graduated as such in 1859. In less than a year after his graduation, Tchaikovsky felt that he had chosen the wrong career, and so began the arduous task of beginning a new profession - this time in music.

mf
dim.

mp

p

mp

Fine
mf
f
p
D.C. al Fine

Funeral March for A Doll

In 1877 Tchaikovsky was relieved of all financial worries by a wealthy widow, Frau von Meck, who arranged an annuity for him which enabled the composer to devote himself wholly to composition. His letters to this "incomparable friend", whom he never met personally, reveal in words his appreciation for her kindness as well as his sensitive and morbid disposition.

"Funeral March for a Doll" is from an album of twenty-four pieces for children. Most of them are descriptive, such as this one.

cresendo poco a poco

Air

Old French Song

Tchaikovsky demonstrates his ability to harmonize a melody in a most interesting fashion. Be sure to follow the phrasing indications and dynamic markings carefully. In measures 17-20 care must be taken to play the melody in the right hand very legato while playing the notes in the hand staccato.

p
mf
p

Serenade No. 4

The word Serenade literally means evening song. As originally intended, it meant music to be sung or played at nightfall, preferably beneath the window of an admired lady friend. Imagine how flattering to a young lady such a performance would be!

Of course, the instruments employed had to be portable, so lutes, guitars, mandolins, and members of the violin family were the favorite instruments.

This piece was originally written for two violins and cello -a perfect combination for portable, romantic music.

sf
sf
mf

Melody

(Minuetto)

The key of A flat major is usually a difficult key in which to play. However, this piece is an easy one!

For the student's benefit, the trills have been written out in the manner to be played. (Located in measures 7 and 15.)

Minuet in E Flat

The minuet was a favorite musical form Mozart. He wrote a great many of them. Haydn and Beethoven also employed this form in numerous compositions, particularly in symphonies and string quartets. The minuet was originally designed for dancing and became fashionable about the middle of the 17th century.

Moonlight Sonata

(Op. 27, No.2)

Until the coming of his deafness, it is probable that a stable part of Beethoven's income was derived from teaching. His reputation as a concert artist and composer attracted many pupils, some of them high ranking nobility.

Among his gifted pupils was Countess Giulia Guicciardi. They became close friends - close enough for the tale of an engagement made and broken to gain acceptance. It is to her that Beethoven dedicated the beautiful "Moonlight Sonata."

p
dim.

pp
p

mp

p

rit.

a tempo

pp

cresc.
pp
p
p

p
pp
pp
p
poco rit.
pp
pp

Adagio

This Adagio movement is from a set of Eleven Viennese Serenades for two violins and cello. The left hand plays the part of cello, and the right hand represents the two violins.

Waltz

When greatness in music is thought of, the first name to come to mind is usually Beethoven. He came from humble heritage but through unlimited musical gifts, perseverance and strength of character, rose to musical heights that have never been surpassed.

Ludwig van Beethoven was born December 16, 1770, in the city of Bonn, Germany. He died in Vienna in 1827 at the age of fifty-seven.

The following piece is from a set of German dances.

Minuet (G minor)

This G minor minuet is based on the same musical form as the previous one in G major. Both have two sections, each section containing 16 measures. This is called Binary Form, which means that a piece is divided into two distinct or contrasting sections.

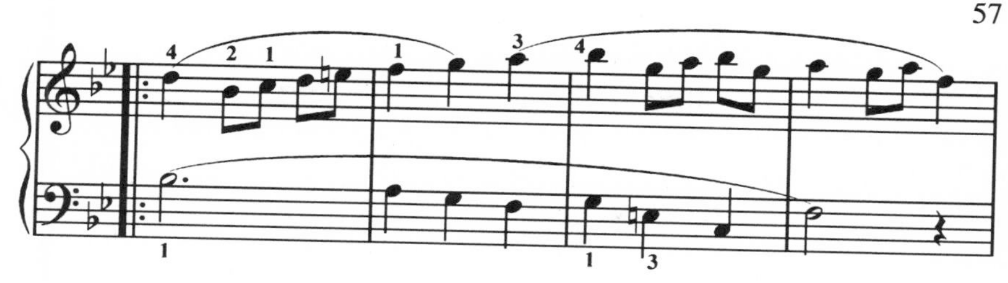
4
2
1
1
3
4
1
1
1
3

1
1
5
2
1
2
1
1
4
5
1

4
1
5
1
1
3
1
3
1

1
1
1
4
5
2
1
2
5
1
5

March

Marches were originally associated with the military but after a time, began to make their appearance in music for the stage, the orchestra and keyboard instruments. Many famous composers have written marches including Handel, Haydn, Beethoven, Verdi, and Wagner.

This particular march is one of the many short teaching pieces Bach wrote for his second wife. It is from a book of pieces in manuscript entitled, *Clavier Book for Anna Magdalena*.

Minuet (C minor)

Many stories regarding Bach have been told. One of particular interest concerns Frederick the Great, King of Prussia.

In 1747 the King, who was a great admirer of Bach and his music, sent an invitation for him to visit the royal palace. When a chamberlain came into the room telling the King that Bach had just arrived by stagecoach, the King suddenly rose from his seat and announced excitedly, "Gentlemen, old Bach has arrived." All previous commitments were cancelled as the King and his guests listened for hours to the King of musicians.

Minuet

(from "Don Giovanni")

Wolfgang Amadeus Mozart, one of the most remarkable child prodigies in all music history, was born in Salzburg, Germany, January 27, 1756. His interest in music began at the age of three. His father, Leopold, a professional violinist, was quick to notice how eagerly young Wolfgang listened to his eight year old sister's music lessons, and how he would amuse himself afterwards by playing harmonious intervals at the keyboard for hours. Also noticed was his ability to remember music that he heard.

A Minuet is a dance form, written in 3/4 or 3/8 time. The chief characteristics are nobility and grace. Like other great composers, Mozart wrote many Minuets.

mp
f
f

Allegro

This little solo was written on March 4, 1762, only eight days after Mozart's sixth birthday. Even in this early composition the "Mozart Style" is noticeable and gives an indication of truly great music he would write in forthcoming years.

Mozart and his sister, Maria Anna, five years older than he, were both child prodigies. When Wolfgang was only six and Maria Anna eleven, their father started taking them on concert tours to such cities as Munich, Brussels, Frankfort, Vienna and Paris. Public concerts were given, besides their playing for the nobility at various courts. Their playing was always received with great enthusiasm.

1
3
1
1
4
1
3
5
4
5
4
4
2
4

Larghetto

Two of Mozart's musical gifts which displayed themselves in early childhood were absolute pitch and a remarkable musical memory.

A musician with absolute pitch is able to identify notes, or combinations of them, simply by hearing them played. No other aid is necessary.

Absolute pitch is very useful to the concert performer who plays from memory- the accurate ear ever guiding the fingers.

Proof of Mozarts amazing musical memory was once demonstrated by his hearing a long composition at the Sistine Chapel in Rome and then writing it down from memory. He was 14 years of age at the time. This feat made a great sensation.

mf
mp

Theme From the Magic Flute

("O Cara Armonia")

This little melody, or theme, is from Mozart's magic opera, "The Magic Flute." The opera contains many humorous situations (beside a few frightening ones) and numerous tricks and optical illusions occur in the course of its performance. This opera is one of Mozart's greatest masterpieces.

Andante

Mozart began giving concerts at the age of six and continued to do so for the remainder of his life. Audiences were always much impressed by his performances - some extremely so.

At one concert in Italy, his hearers were superstitious enough to attribute his marvelous execution to the charm of a ring on his finger. He then laid the ring aside, and their astonishment knew no bounds. Mozart was about 14 years of age at the time.

Arie des Papageno

(from "The Magic Flute")

In the opera, "The Magic Flute", Papageno plays the part of a happy-go-lucky young man who somehow always manages to get himself into amusing predicaments. Throughout the opera he carries a little musical instrument consisting of tubes of different lengths bound together, called Pipes of Pan. The sound and manner of playing is similar to little paraffin blowpipes sometimes sold in stores that sell novelties.

In this piece you will notice that little five-note figure of the Pan Pipes is imitated four times.

(pipes)
8va
8va

Andante Cantabile

(Theme from Violin Concerto No. 4)

In 1775, when he was nineteen years of age, Mozart wrote his five marvelous violin concertos. These he performed at the court in Salzburg where he was employed. Though the violin was not his favorite instrument, he must have played it well. In a letter dated October 18, 1777, his father wrote to him: "You have no idea how well you play the violin, if you would only do yourself justice and play with boldness, spirit and fire, as if you were the finest violinist in Europe."

Ländler

Though Beethoven had a kind and loving mother, his childhood was difficult. The principal cause of domestic difficulties was the father who, though a musician himself, attempted to exploit young Ludwig's musical gifts. Worst of all, he was an intemperate man, thriftless, and a poor provider.

The Ländler is a national dance, popular in Austria, Bavaria and Bohemia. It is similar to a waltz, but the tempo should be a little slower. Mozart and Schubert also wrote Ländlers.

mf
p

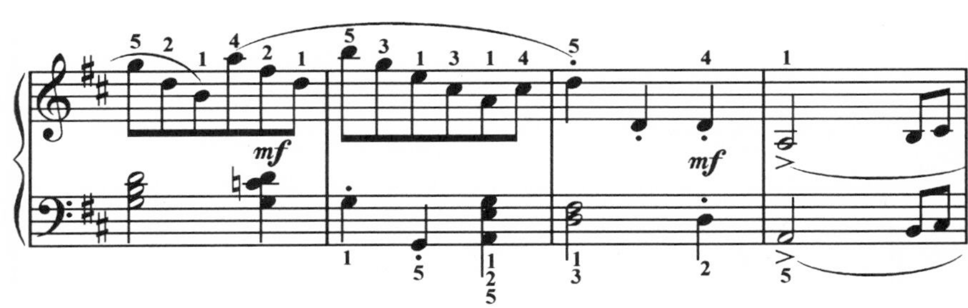
mf
mf

mp
mf

f

Minuet in G

This page has been left blank to avoid awkward page turns.

Russian Song

In 1865 Tchaikovsky completed his musical studies at the Moscow Conservatory and was immediately offered the post of professor of harmony. Through the pay was only moderate, the honor of the position greatly enhanced Tchaikovsky's reputation as a musician and composer.

The piece, "Russian Song" is folk-like in character. It is based on a simple melody to which the composer has added ever-changing harmonizations to make it a beautiful composition.

Serenade Melancolique

Tchaikovsky has been called the "symphonic apostle of gloom," and anyone familiar with the Sixth Symphony or music for the ballet "Swan Lake" might readily agree to that assessment. But the statement is not completely true, for much of his music is of a cheerful nature, such as found in the *Fourth Symphony*, the *Nutcracker Suite* and pieces for piano.

Serenade Melancolique was originally written for solo violin with orchestral accompaniment. The principal theme is very beautiful. It is presented here, transcribed for the piano.

Morning Prayer

From his fortieth year onward Tchaikovsky's popularity as a composer continued to grow throughout Russia and the world. His principal orchestral works and operas were receiving performances by some of the best musical organizations. Now the composer could enjoy the fruits of his labor.

However, in 1893 Tchaikovsky contracted cholera from drinking unboiled water while an epidemic was raging in Moscow, which resulted in his death at the age of fifty-three.

f
mf

Surprise Symphony

(Theme from Symphony No. 94)

"Surprise Symphony" is the familiar name given to Haydn's "Symphony Number 94." It is so-called because of the loud chord in the slow movement, said to have been written in the piece to awaken sleepy English audiences. Haydn's own explanation was, "This will make the ladies jump."

* The surprise chord.

mf

pp
dim.
p

mf
f
pp

Andante Grazioso

Even as a youngster, music history tells us, Haydn was "always full of fun and inclined to practical jokes." Once, at school, he was discovered doing a balancing act on some high scaffolding for the entertainment of his school fellows. Another time he cut off the pigtail of an unsuspecting student with a new pair of scissors! Although Haydn was a deeply religious person, his happy disposition and love of practical jokes never left him. He once remarked to an old friend that "a mischievous fit comes over one sometimes that is perfectly beyond control." Life was never dull for Joseph Haydn.

dim.

Romanze

(from Symphony No.85 "La Reine")

"Romanze", Romance, which is the English equivalent, is a rather vague term in music where the characteristics are those of personal sentiment and expression. Many composers have used the word, Romance, for the titles of pieces including Mozart, Beethoven, Schumann and Wieniawski, to name a few.

cresc.

mf
pp

p

Joyful

Haydn was born in a little house at the end of the market place at Rohrau, Austria. From such a humble beginning came one of the world's greatest composers and one, more than any other, who would greatly influence two musical geniuses in his own lifetime - Mozart and Beethoven.

Do not take the word VIVACE, which appears at the beginning of this piece, too literally.

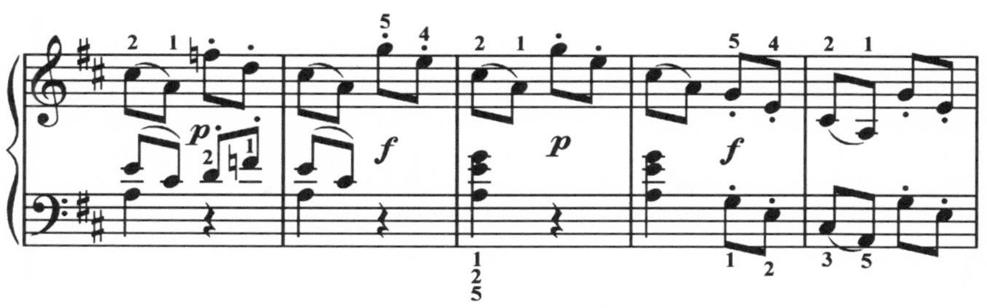
p
f
p
f

p
cresc.
poco rit.
dim.

a tempo
p
mp
cresc.

f

Minuet

(from "The Military Symphony No. 100")

Like most of the great composers, Haydn's musical training began early. Music lessons were commenced when he was six years of age. Learning came easily to him, and he progressed rapidly. When he was eight years of age, he was accepted as a choir boy at St. Stephen's Cathedral in Vienna where musical studies continued until he was 16.

pp
f
f

EXCELLENCE IN MUSIC
MEL BAY®
Since 1947